GO INLAND!

A young person's guide to
Inland Waterways

RYA Go Inland!

Words and Illustrations by: Claudia Myatt
Technical Editor: Samantha Clarke, Principal & Chief
Instructor, Canalboat Training & Concoform Marine

© Claudia Myatt 2008
First Published 2008

The Royal Yachting Association
RYA House
Ensign Way
Hamble
Southampton
SO31 4YA

Tel: 0845 345 0400
Fax: 0845 345 0329
E-mail: publications@rya.org.uk
Web: www.rya.org.uk

ISBN: 9781905104413
RYA Order Code: G54

A CIP record of this book is available from the British Library

Note: While all reasonable care has been taken in the preparation of this book, the publisher takes no responsibility for the use of the methods or products or contracts described in the book.

Cover Design: Claudia Myatt
Typeset: Creativebyte
Proofreading and indexing: Alan Thatcher
Printed through: World Print

FOREWORD

The delights of our inland waterways were apparent to me from a very young age and their charm remains with me to this day. I lived on a narrowboat for a number of years, and the waterways have always offered me an escape from my busy life as an actor.

The hundreds of miles of canals and waterways which criss-cross this country not only give me the freedom to travel many miles in peace, but also transport me back to a more leisurely time when nothing was done in a hurry.

Our waterways carry us to some of the most tranquil places imaginable and everyone, young and old, deserves the chance to discover their magic.

Go Inland! is a perfect introduction to our waterways and teaches you how to go about the everyday business of travelling along them in a safe manner. The illustrations will also keep you smiling all the way through.

I can't help but feel that children of all ages will benefit from reading this book as many of the tips are excellent whether you are seven or seventy seven.

I was always keen to encourage my own children onto the water and I only wish such an excellent book had been available when they were learning the ropes.

David Suchet

CONTENTS

INTRODUCTION

When you cruise the inland waterways you discover the secret heart of the country. You'll be amazed at how many places you can get to by boat, and how many different things there are to see and do along the way. You'll go through busy cities and quiet countryside, along tiny canals or wide rivers, even lakes. There are places to stop and explore, and you'll learn about locks, bridges and tunnels.

Travelling slowly means you can get up close to all kinds of wildlife and you'll see far more than you ever would by car. The best bit is that you don't have to go home at the end of the day because you'll have your home with you!

Being afloat is special—if you want to know why, try it yourself (or ask a duck!).

Claudia Myatt

INLAND WATERS

These are some of the things you'll find on a cruise along rivers and canals. Canals are man made and rivers are natural, though most rivers have been modified by locks and weirs to make them easier for boats to navigate.

STAIRCASE LOCKS are a series of locks that take you up or down a steep hill. Clever engineering!

AQUEDUCTS carry canals over a valley - some are quite small, but some, are spectacular. Don't look down!

There are plenty of **BRIDGES** to go under, especially on canals, from simple brick arches (usually a tight fit!) lifting or swing bridges.

All canals and some rivers have a **TOWPATH** along one side; this was how horses used to pull the barges in the days before diesel engines. Towpaths are great for walks and for mooring up.

WINDING HOLES are where boats can turn round - useful when the boats are longer than the canal is wide!

JOLLY BOATMAN

REFRESHMENTS! Rivers and canals have waterside pubs with moorings so you can tie up and step ashore for lunch!

Waterways don't just go through pretty countryside, they go through cities and towns too, so you can get right to the heart of a big city without the traffic hassle! Many rivers and canals are all linked up, so you could start a journey on the tiniest canal deep in the countryside and go all the way to the sea.

TUNNELS If there was a hill in the way of the canal builders, they would sometimes tunnel through it. Some canal tunnels are very long and very dark!

MARINAS and boatyards have space to moor your boat, take on fuel and empty holding tanks, as well as maintenance and repairs.

LAKES can be part of inland waterways, especially when they are linked to the canal and river system. Lakes (or 'broads' in Norfolk) are good for different kinds of boating, including sailing.

You'll come across **LOCKS** on rivers and canals. They were built to carry boats up or down hill. Some canal locks are very narrow - they just fit one boat - and some, like those in the European canal system, are enormous!

WEIRS help to control a river's flow. They have sluice gates which can be closed if water levels need to be adjusted. Marker buoys make sure boats don't get too close!

Waterways have their own set of road **SIGNS** - this one means there's a lock ahead. You can look up the most well known ones at the back of this book.

LOCK

What sort of boats use the inland waterways? Here are a few of the main types...

NARROWBOAT

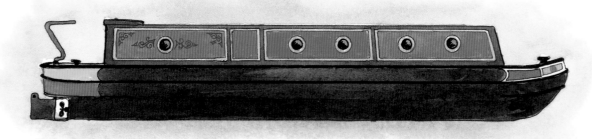

The main thing you'll notice about narrowboats is that they're.... well... narrow! This is because they were designed for the British canal system, so they can't be more than 6'10" wide or 70' long. You'll find narrowboats on canals and rivers, but they're not designed to go to sea.

A traditional narrowboat stern is tiny! When steering, stand in the hatchway for safety. A cruiser stern, usually found on hire boats, is much bigger and often has seating or safety rails at the stern.

TRADITIONAL STERN

SEMI TRADITIONAL STERN

Looks traditional but has more space inside enclosed sides.

CRUISER STERN

SEA-GOING CRUISER

Motor cruisers come in all shapes and sizes; they can't fit on narrow canals but one like this can go on wide canals, rivers, estuaries and out to sea.

RIVER CRUISER ⟶

Smaller motor cruisers like this are found on rivers, estuaries, lakes and wide canals.

DUTCH BARGE

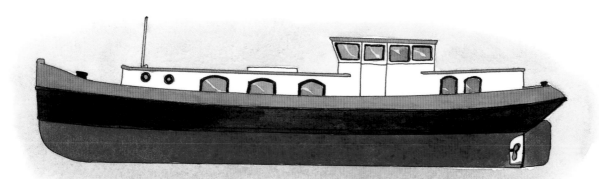

Dutch style barges like this are based on the cargo carrying boats of the European canals and rivers; they tend to be big and beamy (wide) so they make great floating homes. You'll find these on the bigger rivers and canals, especially in Europe, and they're also popular as houseboats.

OTHER TYPES OF BOAT Boats come in all shapes and sizes, especially on rivers, but here are just a few to look out for....

SAILING DINGHY...
If the river is wide
enough to sail on!

ELECTRIC LAUNCH - so quiet you won't
hear it coming!

FERRIES, FLOATING RESTAURANTS and DAY TRIPPER
boats—wave and they'll always wave back!

KAYAK - probably the smallest
boat on the river.

ROWING SKIFF
- long, lean and
very fast!

On rivers and canals you may be close to land but being on the water is a different world with its own special language.

Here are some boaty words to get you in the mood.....

These basic terms apply to every sort of boat, so this is a good place to start.

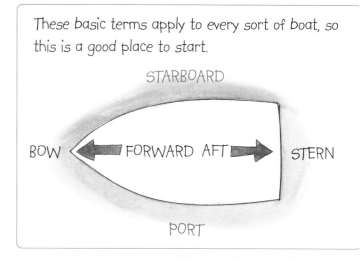

STARBOARD

BOW ← FORWARD AFT → STERN

PORT

NARROWBOAT

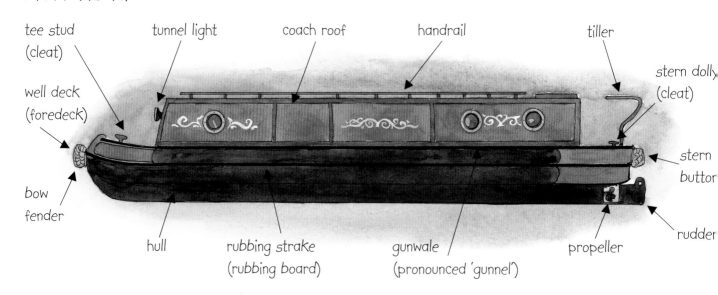

tee stud (cleat)

well deck (foredeck)

bow fender

tunnel light

coach roof

handrail

tiller

stern dolly (cleat)

stern button

hull

rubbing strake (rubbing board)

gunwale (pronounced 'gunnel')

propeller

rudder

MOTOR CRUISER

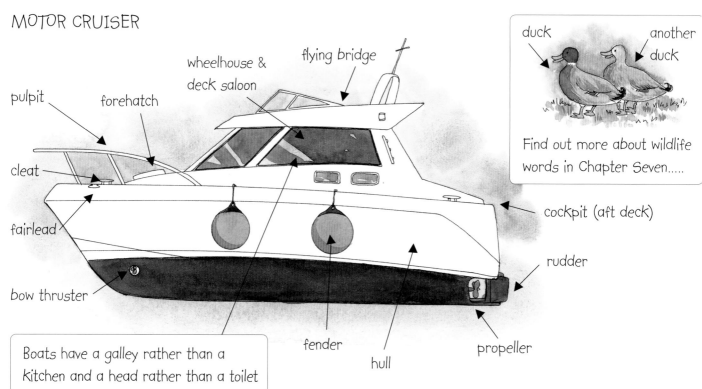

pulpit

forehatch

wheelhouse & deck saloon

flying bridge

cleat

fairlead

bow thruster

fender

hull

cockpit (aft deck)

rudder

propeller

duck

another duck

Find out more about wildlife words in Chapter Seven.....

Boats have a galley rather than a kitchen and a head rather than a toilet

Being water wise means taking care of your own safety. Start by always wearing a lifejacket or buoyancy aid when you're on or near the water - make a habit of it and never forget that water can be dangerous as well as fun!

MAKE SURE IT FITS!
Wearing a lifejacket that doesn't fit properly is as bad as not wearing one at all.

If there are leg straps fitted, make sure you use them.

BAD IDEA

GOOD IDEA

A lifejacket will keep you fully supported with your head clear of the water. It's quite bulky but essential for non swimmers and small children.

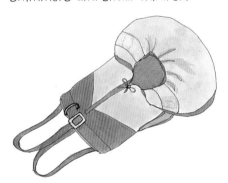

An automatic lifejacket like this will inflate if you hit the water - easy to wear, good for older children and adults.

A buoyancy aid like this is not a lifejacket, but it helps you to stay afloat. It's less bulky than a lifejacket, good for confident swimmers and older children.

Just because you're wearing a lifejacket, don't get careless - being water wise means never having to put your lifejacket to the test. Falling in is unpleasant as well as dangerous - rubbish and sharp objects get thrown into rivers and canals, currents can be strong and there can also be a risk of catching nasty diseases.

The golden rule of any kind of boating is ALWAYS HOLD ON tight!

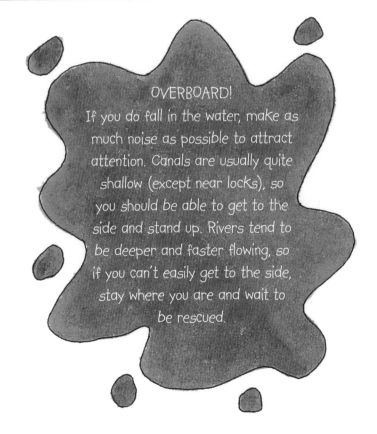

OVERBOARD!
If you do fall in the water, make as much noise as possible to attract attention. Canals are usually quite shallow (except near locks), so you should be able to get to the side and stand up. Rivers tend to be deeper and faster flowing, so if you can't easily get to the side, stay where you are and wait to be rescued.

You'll be spending a lot of time outdoors, so take plenty of comfortable clothes for all kinds of weather. Avoid clothes with extra baggy bits or trailing trousers which can get caught on boat fittings and trip you up! The same goes for dangly jewellery and long hair - especially around locks.

Zip up trouser pockets are great for phones, keys and cameras.

WHAT'S AFOOT?

The right shoes are important as you need to be able to move quickly and safely around the boat, which may have narrow side decks. Choose shoes with plenty of grip. Flip flops or any backless shoes are a bad idea - you'll end up losing one or both over the side.

GOOD IDEA

BAD IDEA

Wellies might seem practical on a boat but they're not - if you fall in the water they'll weigh you down. They're not good for moving quickly around the boat, either.

You'll need waterproofs—even if it doesn't rain, you may need to go through a dripping tunnel!

Don't forget sun hat and sun cream, too.

Well, I'm ready!

Other useful stuff to take:
- Camera
- Binoculars
- Games and books
- Spare batteries

For the activities in Chapter Six you'll need:
- Exercise book, sketch book, pencils and crayons (with paints, brushes, ruler, scissors, glue stick, stiff card and compasses if there's room!)

I'm ready too!

HOW IT ALL BEGAN

Before you step on board, stop and think about the water you're about to cruise on. If it's a canal, how did it get there? Who built it and why did they go to all that trouble? If you're on a river, where does it go to and how long has it been sailed on?

Read this bit before you start and you'll impress your family by knowing all kinds of amazing facts. You'll also be able to explain some of the things you'll see along the way.

Imagine a world before cars, motorways, roads, planes or trains. All you had were horse drawn carts and bumpy tracks, so moving heavy stuff around was slow and difficult. A journey that today takes a few hours in a car would take several days by horse and cart.

Once the industrial revolution got going in the 19th century, there was a need for a better way of carrying large amounts of cargo, especially coal to power all the new factories.

Well, it wasn't here last time!

RIVERS TO THE RESCUE

Rivers are nature's highways and they've been used for transport ever since early man noticed that a log floats and used it to paddle to the other side of the river. But rivers can be tricky; fast flowing after storms, too narrow or winding, with strong currents or shifting sandbanks. And they don't always go where you want them to!

So rivers were often CANALISED, improved to make them easier to sail on—like a bypass round a tricky bit, a short cut, or an extension to reach a town. Canals were dug as highways for boats, joining up rivers and linking towns. Have a look at the maps at each end of this book to see how the canal system linked important towns with each other and with the sea.

HORSE POWER!

In wide rivers, estuaries and at sea, boats used the wind to get around. On narrow rivers and canals heavy boats needed a horse, or occasionally a team of men, to pull them along. This is why all canals were built with a towpath alongside them. A horse could pull 2 tonnes of coal on land, but 50 tonnes on water! Not only was it efficient for heavy loads but gave a really smooth ride for fragile goods like pottery.

GET DIGGING!

Most of the British canals were built in the 18th century to move heavy goods like coal between the expanding industrial towns.

It was difficult, expensive and slow work; there were no bulldozers or power tools, just lots of strong men with shovels and pickaxes. Canals were known as 'cuts' or 'navigations' so the men who built them were called 'navvies' - a word still used for labourers today.

Once the trench was dug, it was lined with puddled clay - a very watery slushy mixture - to stop the water draining out.

HOW DID CANALS GET OVER HILLS?

One thing you'll notice about water is that it always flows downhill, which is a problem if you want your canal to go over hills. The first canals followed the contours of the land as much as possible. They were winding like rivers and all on one level so the water wouldn't fall out.

As canal builders got smarter, they used locks, tunnels, embankments and aqueducts to get their canals through hilly landscapes and across valleys. This made the journey time shorter for boats and meant that goods could be delivered faster.

WHERE DID THE WATER COME FROM?

Digging a huge ditch is one thing—getting it to fill with water is quite another. Sometimes the rivers linked to canals would supply the water, but if the canal went over a hill, engineers had to build a reservoir at the highest point, or a pumping station, to keep the level of the canal as constant as possible.

LOCKS are like steps in a river or canal – a way for boats to go up and down hill without all the water falling out. You'll find out how to use them in the next chapter, but here's the basic idea......

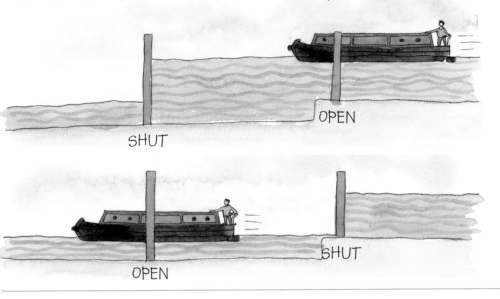

SHUT

OPEN

OPEN

SHUT

Once the boat is in the lock chamber both gates are shut. Sluices (little gates) are opened to let water in (if the boat is going uphill) or out (if the boat is going downhill). When the level inside the lock is the same as outside, the gate is opened to let the boat out.

STAIRCASE LOCKS

If the hill is quite steep, there may be a series of locks instead of one great big one. When the top gate of one lock forms the bottom gate of the next lock this is called a STAIRCASE LOCK.

The problem with locks is that they lose a lot of water every time a boat goes through, so a series of locks is less wasteful of water than one big one.

The Bingley Five Rise, on the Leeds & Liverpool Canal, is short and steep - it takes boats up and down a staggering 60 feet.

OK – if you're so smart, you work it out!

Lock gates have to hold back a lot of heavy water - how do they do it?

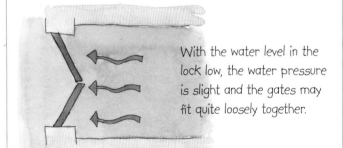

With the water level in the lock low, the water pressure is slight and the gates may fit quite loosely together.

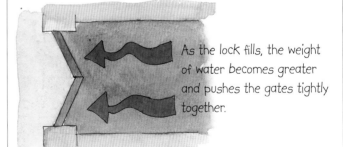

As the lock fills, the weight of water becomes greater and pushes the gates tightly together.

It was that 15th century brain-box Leonardo da Vinci, who designed the MITRE GATE. The V-shape made by the two gates means that the more the water pushes against them, the tighter together they fit.

It works so well that even the biggest lock gates in the world still use this basic design.

Another way of getting canals through hills was by digging a tunnel. This was difficult and dangerous so tunnels were usually built as small as possible - only just big enough for one boat (or sometimes two) to get through at a time. There was often no room for a towpath. Some tunnels had chains along the walls to pull the boat through, but usually it had to be propelled through the tunnel by LEGGING. Two men lay on their back on a plank, one each side of the boat, walking the boat along the tunnel walls. Imagine doing this in a long, dark, dripping tunnel... yeuk!

In long tunnels, professional 'leggers' were paid to help boats through. In the 1790s a legger at the Dudley Tunnel got paid 3 shillings and sixpence for the gruelling three hour one way journey (that's about 17pence!).

Many of the original tunnels have been restored and you'll still use them today. Now boats have engines you won't need to do any legging, but you'll still find going through a canal tunnel an interesting experience!

The longest tunnel in Britain is the Standedge Tunnel at 3.25 miles long. It is also the highest (196 metres above sea level) as it crosses the Pennines near Huddersfield. Digging started in 1794 and the tunnel took 17 years – with a little help from a rather clever engineer called Thomas Telford.

GHOSTLY GOINGS ON
Several tunnels are said to be haunted - probably because they're dark, damp and spooky.

The Harecastle Tunnel on the Trent and Mersey Canal is famous for its headless ghost called Kit Crewbucket. Even in recent times, boats using the tunnel have reported seeing the lights of an old cargo boat coming towards them just as they're about to go into the tunnel... but then the boat disappears...

I don't care if you are afraid of heights, I wish you'd steer with your eyes open!

It wasn't just hills that gave canal designers a headache; canals had to be built as level as possible, so valleys were a problem too. Aqueducts are bridges that carry a canal across a valley - over a river, a road, or another canal - and they do this without spilling any water!

Some aqueducts are so small you hardly notice them, but some are really impressive, like the Pontcysyllte in North Wales (say 'pontkersulty' and you won't be far wrong), which is 1007' (307m) long and 126' (38m) at its highest part. It's the tallest and longest aqueduct in the UK.

If you think that's clever, there's more - the BARTON SWING AQUEDUCT carries the Bridgewater Canal over the Manchester Ship Canal. When a big ship comes down the Ship Canal, gates at either end of the aqueduct close to keep the water in and the entire bridge swings around a central pier. The aqueduct opened in 1893 and is still in use today!

PULLING THE PLUG - to repair the 200 year old Pontcysyllte aqueduct, gates at either end of the bridge were closed and the plug pulled out to let 1.5 million litres of water cascade onto the river below.

Look, mum...

Canals were the main roads of the day, carrying goods and people all over the country. But in the 19th century some smarty-pants invented railways, which eventually became quicker and more economical than the canal boats. In the last days of canal trade, whole families lived and worked on their boats to try and save money; cabins were tiny as most of the space on the boat was needed for cargo.

By the 1960s British canals were empty. They fell into disrepair and became overgrown; nobody looked after locks and bridges and many of the tunnels fell in. In the 1970s a few people decided

this was a shame, so they got together and started to restore the neglected canal system. Teams of volunteers worked hard to clear the undergrowth, let the water back in and restore the locks, tunnels and bridges. This work is still going on, but the UK now enjoys over 3,000 miles of navigable waterways once more.

There is still plenty more work to be done - you'll find more information on canal restoration in Chapter Seven.

Rivers and canals are once again in full use by people like you cruising for fun, enjoying the waterways and the interesting places they take you to. As roads get busier and fuel gets more expensive, the history of canals and rivers may come full circle and they'll start to carry more cargo again.

WELCOME ABOARD

CREW JOB LIST

Handle mooring lines and fenders and stow them neatly

Move around the boat safely

Steer the boat without bumping into anything!

Avoid falling overboard!

With your bags stowed and your lifejacket on, you're ready to be a useful crew. When it's time to set off, your first job will be bringing in the mooring lines, which on a canal or still water is quite easy to do ...

When there's no current, boats only need a bow line and stern line to tie them to the bank.

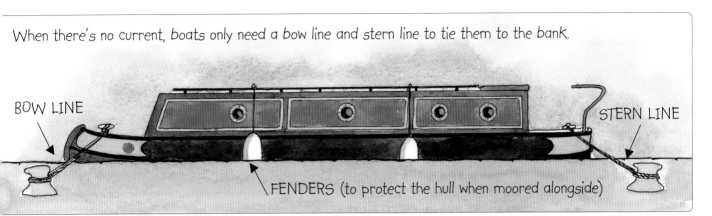

BOW LINE

STERN LINE

FENDERS (to protect the hull when moored alongside)

The skipper will tell you which line he wants to untie first. Mind your fingers!

Try to keep the rope clear of the water as you step on board.

If the boat is tied to mooring stakes, remember to bring them on board with you!

Er, dad...!

Don't let any ropes trail in the water or they could get tangled in the propeller.

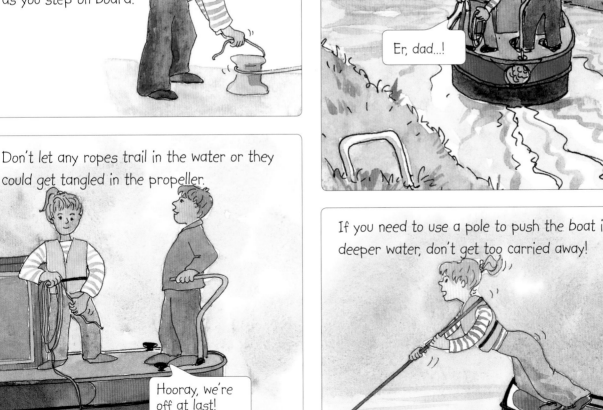

Hooray, we're off at last!

heehee!

If you need to use a pole to push the boat into deeper water, don't get too carried away!

heehee!

On a river where there is moving water, a boat needs extra mooring lines to keep it safe. As well as a bow and stern line, the skipper will put out springs to stop the boat moving forwards or backwards in the current.

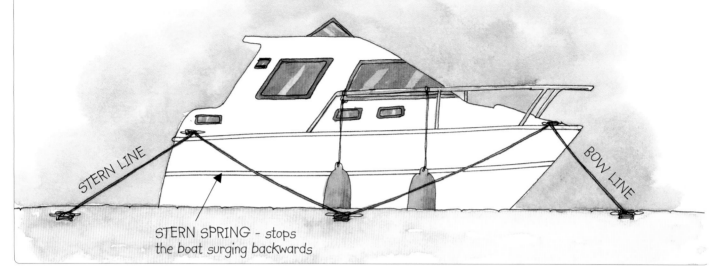

STERN LINE

BOW LINE

STERN SPRING - stops
the boat surging backwards

Casting off mooring lines in moving water requires planning, as the boat will start to move as soon as the ropes are untied.

Leaving a quayside you can use the mooring posts to put the rope 'on a slip' like this, so it can be controlled from on board...

... then you can quickly pull in the slack as the boat moves away.

STAY SAFE!

Learn how to move around the boat safely. Side decks on most boats are narrow, so get into the habit of holding on securely all the time. On a narrowboat it is usually easier to get to the foredeck by going through the cabin rather than round the outside.

Both narrowboats and cruisers have handrails along the side decks to help you.

WATER WISDOM! Don't keep mobile phones or other valuables in your pockets (unless you've got zip up pockets). They can easily fall out when you're bending over mooring lines.

Whose mobile have you got?

Not sure... says it's a 'seamens'...

Once you've cast off, there are a few jobs to do before you can relax. Coiling and stowing mooring lines is important, as they need to be safely stowed and not tangled up next time they're needed!

HOW TO COIL A ROPE

Whether the line is being left on deck ready for next time, or stowed away in a locker, it's important to coil it properly so that it doesn't tangle. Here's how it goes.....

1. If you're right handed, hold the coils in your left hand (and if you're left handed hold them in your right hand).

2 The secret of a good coil is to twist your right hand outward as you make each coil. This stops the coil from kinking up.

3 To keep the coils the same length, use the width of your arm for each coil.

Oops! How not to coil a rope.... If it ends up looking like this, you've been forgetting to twist your hand outwards as you go.

Go back to step two and have another go.

FINISHING OFF.....

If your rope is staying on deck ready for the next time you moor up, coil from the fixed end first or you won't be able to shake out the kinks. Leave the coil neatly on deck without any bits trailing over the side of the boat.

If the skipper asks you to put the rope away in a locker, you need to tie off the coil so that it doesn't come undone.

Finish it off like this and pull tight.

Boats use fenders when moored up to stop the hull getting scratched. These need to be brought in once you're under way—either untied and put away in a locker (don't drop them over the side!) ....

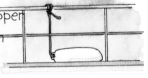

...........or for shorter trips your skipper might ask you to leave them tied on and brought in on deck like this.

You'll find out all about which knots to use and how to tie them in the next chapter.

How to steer

STEERING THE BOAT (taking the helm) takes a bit of practice, but you'll soon get the feel of it.

The most common mistake is to turn the wheel or tiller too far. You usually only need very tiny adjustments to keep the boat on course. In a narrow canal or river steering in a straight line is harder than you think to start with!

I think I'm getting the hang of it.....!

WHEEL STEERING

Most cruisers have wheel steering, so you simply turn the wheel the way you want the boat to go. Make small adjustments of the wheel to start with to get used to how the boat responds.

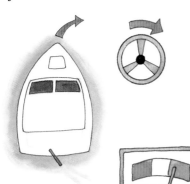

The flow of water over the rudder makes the boat turn. There will probably be a dial on the control panel to show the position of the rudder so that you know how far you need to turn the wheel to bring it back to the centre again.

TILLER STEERING

Tiller steering can take a bit of getting used to, as the boat goes in the opposite direction to the way you move the tiller. Here's how it works.....

Tiller to port moves the rudder (and the boat) to starboard (right).......

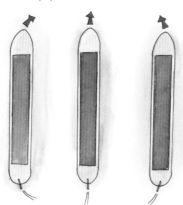

Tiller to starboard moves the rudder (and the boat) to port (left).......

The boat will carry on turning after you've brought the tiller back to the centre—you'll soon learn to bring it back to the middle just before you think you need to!

ENGINE CONTROLS

Boat engine controls are simple. They have three positions —forward, reverse and neutral.

SINGLE ENGINE

TWIN ENGINE

Get to know how they work, so that when you're on the helm you can slow down or speed up without taking your eyes off where you're going.

GETTING A GRIP.....

If steering in a straight line is hard, you'll find turning takes a bit of getting used to. This is because water is slippery stuff, and most boats turn around a pivot point about a third of the way back from the bow.

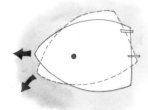

This means that when you turn the wheel or tiller, the stern will move more than the bow.

On a long narrowboat, the stern will move a lot more than the bow. It helps if you think about where the back of the boat is going as well as the front!

TWIN ENGINED CRUISERS

Bigger cruisers have two engines and two rudders, so a skipper can use the engine controls if he needs to make some tight turns....

A burst of forward on the port engine turns the boat to starboard.........

A burst of forward on the starboard engine turns the boat to port.

Both engines together drive the boat forward....

Forward on one engine and reverse on the other will turn the boat in circles!

GOING BACKWARDS

Most boats don't steer easily in reverse. Don't use too much power or the pressure of water on the rudder will hold it flat and the tiller will swing out of control. On a narrowboat, increase speed very gently as you reverse; on a cruiser use short bursts of power.

For tiller steering, face the back of the boat and turn the tiller opposite to the way you want to go. For wheel steering you'll need to face forwards but look over your shoulder to check your course. Don't forget to keep an eye on what the bow of the boat is doing! If the bow is swinging the wrong way, steer in the opposite direction to get back on course.

On British canals the speed limit is 4 miles per hour (just over 6Km per hour); on European canals it varies from 5km to 8km per hour. On rivers there will be speed limit signs and the current will affect your speed, but more about that [c] the end of the chapter.

Most of the time you'll be travelling at a relaxed pace, well within the limits!

REASONS TO GO SLOW....

Just because the speed limit is 4mph doesn't mean you have to cruise at 4mph! There are lots of reasons to go even slower......

- passing other boats
- passing moored boats
- passing fishermen
- going under a narrow bridge
- going into a lock
- coming to a bend
- approaching a place to moor
- if your wash is disturbing the river bank

WHAT'S THE HURRY?

Get into the relaxed waterways lifestyle, wave and smile at everyone you pass. If you have to wait at a lock, be patient and see it as the opportunity to make new friends!

How do you know if you're going too fast? Pay attention to your surroundings - if the banks are awash and the ducks are getting stressed, you're going too fast whatever it says on the dial!

WATCH OUT FOR WIND!

A strong wind can blow your boat sideways. Turn the bow into the wind enough to keep you on course.

Keep an eye on where the whole boat is going, not where the bow is pointing!

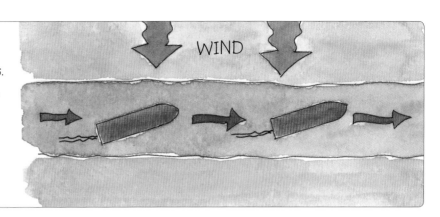

REASONS NOT TO GO SLOW

There are times when you'll need a burst of power. When a boat is stopped, there's no movement of water over the rudder so your steering won't work!

It is also difficult to make the boat turn when going really slowly. On a narrowboat increase speed gently; on a cruiser use a quick burst of power to help you make a tight turn.

WHERE ARE THE BRAKES?

There aren't any! Putting the engine into neutral will stop the propeller turning but it doesn't stop the boat, which will carry on moving for some time. The heavier the boat, the more she will 'carry way'. If you need to stop quickly, a few moments in neutral followed by a burst of reverse power should do the trick.

STOPPING ALONGSIDE A QUAY OR BANK

On a canal where there is no current, head in bow first then turn the tiller or wheel to bring the stern in. Go as slowly as you can without losing steerage way so that you have a gentle landing!

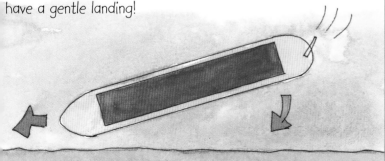

USING THE CURRENT

If you're on a river, the current can be a useful brake. Turning into the current when you come alongside will help to stop the boat, so always moor facing upstream.

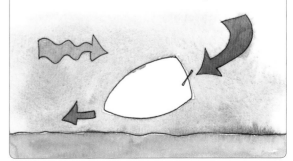

BUT .... Don't relax if you're steering the boat! Remember, you're in charge of where the boat is heading, so you need to be aware of your surroundings, your speed and any hazards coming up.

Even if you're not steering, face the way you're travelling. Sitting on the roof is a really bad idea - as well as being unsafe, it blocks the helmsman's view.

WATCH OUT! Warn the rest of the crew if there's something they need to know—like going under a low bridge, into a tunnel or stopping at a lock.

BAD IDEA

Who, me?

DUCK!

SHALLOW BITS...

Canals and some rivers can be very shallow — going too fast in shallow water will make the stern dig down and disturb all the mud and rubbish at the bottom, which slows you down.

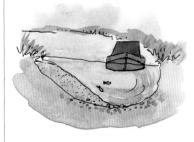

Canals and rivers are shaped like this— deeper in the middle than the sides. The water can often be very shallow near the banks.

On a bend, the deeper water will be on the outside of the bend. Don't take a short cut or you may find yourself stuck on the mud!

GOING AGROUND

If you get stuck in the mud, put the engine into reverse to try and get the stern into deeper water.

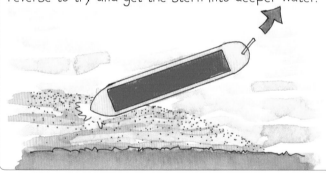

TURNING ROUND

On narrow canals you can't turn round unless you use a WINDING HOLE. Turn the bow of the boat into the hole until it touches the bank. Then turn the tiller the other way (until it is pointing the way you want to go) and put the engine into forward gear. When the stern has come round far enough, put the engine into reverse to take you out of the winding hole and off you go!

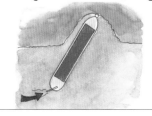

When you're steering the boat you have to know the rules of the road, just like you would in a car. Don't worry, they're quite easy to remember........

DRIVE ON THE RIGHT
Stay on the right side of the channel and pass other boats port to port.

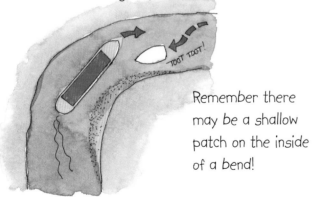

OVERTAKING
You don't usually need to overtake another boat — but if you do, pass on the left and make sure you're not near a bridge or a bend. Keep out of the other boat's way whilst overtaking. (the overtaken boat should slow down to let you pass)

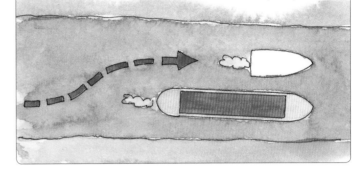

GOING SLOWLY ROUND THE BEND.....
Tight corners can be tricky. Large boats may need to use the whole width of the channel to make the turn. Pass on the wrong side if you need to give them room, giving two toots on the horn which means 'I am turning to port'.

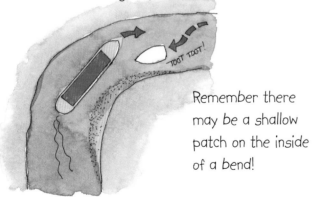

Remember there may be a shallow patch on the inside of a bend!

If you can't see round a bend, give a long toot on your horn to let other boats know you're coming.....

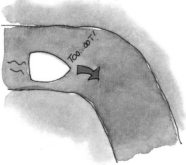

BOATS UNDER SAIL
Sailing boats need to tack (sail a zigzag course) if the wind is against them. Slow down and wait for a chance to go behind them.

NARROW BRIDGES
Slow down well in advance. If the approaching boat is nearer to the bridge than you, let him go through first.

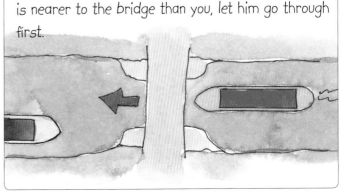

On moving water there is more to think about. A canal has very little current, but on a river the water can be travelling quite fast—especially if there's been a lot of rain! On rivers, too, there are navigation buoys to help to steer around the shallows and sandbanks......

RED AND GREEN BUOYS

On wider rivers you might see red or green buoys, which show where the deep water channel goes.
If you are heading upstream, keep a red buoy to your left (port) and a green buoy to your right (starboard.)

CURRENT AWARE!

If you come to a narrow bit on a river, a boat heading upstream must give way to a boat coming downstream. (remember the boat coming downstream can't stop, but you can!)

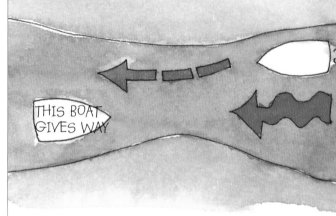

THIS BOAT GIVES WAY

A river current will affect your boat speed—if you are travelling with the current, you'll be faster than if you're travelling against it. Here's some simple maths......

BOAT SPEED 4 KNOTS

CURRENT 2 KNOTS
= 6 KNOTS PROGRESS

BOAT SPEED 4 KNOTS

CURRENT 2 KNOTS
= 2 KNOTS PROGRESS

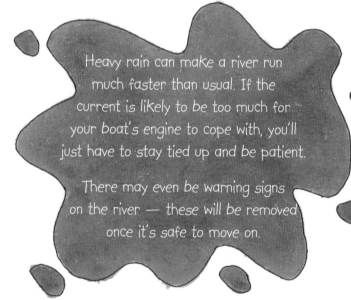

Heavy rain can make a river run much faster than usual. If the current is likely to be too much for your boat's engine to cope with, you'll just have to stay tied up and be patient.

There may even be warning signs on the river — these will be removed once it's safe to move on.

After all those pages of technical stuff you deserve a break, so here's another duck joke before you tackle the next chapter..... (and yes, the duck jokes get even sillier.....)

What time does a duck wake up?

At the quack of dawn!

MOORING TIME

CREW JOB LIST

Help choose a place to stop

Get mooring lines and fenders ready

Take lines ashore safely

Tie the boat up securely and relax!

Life on the waterways is relaxed — and part of the fun is choosing somewhere to stop the boat, either for lunch, to explore, or to stay overnight. Here are a few tips on how to find a good place to moor up.........

ON A CANAL...... Generally you can stop anywhere along the towpath side and stay there for up to 14 days (though some busy areas will have signs showing a time limit). Choose between the peace and quiet of the country or the bustle of a town—but mooring spaces in towns fill up fast, so stop early if you're choosing a popular spot.

ON A RIVER....... The banks of a river are often privately owned, so you can only stop on the towpath side if there are no signs saying 'private'. You'll find public mooring space in towns, villages and outside pubs!

WHERE NOT TO STOP

Avoid mooring near a bridge, tunnel or lock, on private land, opposite a junction or winding hole, or near a sharp bend!

USEFUL SIGNS TO LOOK OUT FOR— and there are lots more at the back of the book.

Stop here when you want to fill your water tanks—but don't stay longer than you need.	This shows a pump out station for your toilet. Again, don't stay longer than you need to.	Mooring is allowed (but there may be a time limit in busy places)	No mooring allowed.

Whether you're stopping for lunch or for the night, the boat needs to be properly secured. The bow and stern line need to be made ready, so you'll be glad you coiled them properly when you set off!

Make sure the coil is tangle free and one end is attached to the boat! Have mooring stakes and mallet ready if you need them....

If the boat has guardrails, make sure the rope is on the outside of the rail like this......

.... and not like this!

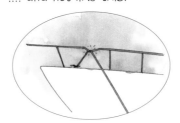

BOATS ARE HEAVY!

When approaching a quayside or river bank, keep your arms and legs well out of the way—chipped paintwork is better than a broken arm.

BAD IDEA

GETTING FENDERS READY

If the fenders are already tied on, simply drop them down over the side of the boat— make sure you know which side they should be on! If you need to tie the fenders on the guardrail, the best knot is a round turn and two half hitches. Here's how it's done.......

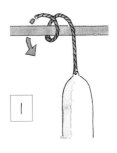

1

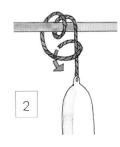

2

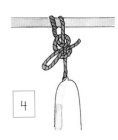

3

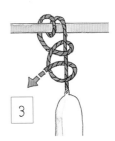

4

If you leave a loop in the last turn, like tying a shoelace, it will be quick to undo.

Don't be a human fender!

GETTING ASHORE

Wait until the boat is alongside the bank and then step ashore.......

.... don't do a flying leap!

CENTRE LINES

It can sometimes be useful to get a line ashore from the middle of the boat. This will hold her in place and give you time to get bow and stern lines sorted out, and is also handy if you need to stop briefly while waiting for a lock.

A narrowboat may already have a rope coiled up on the roof ready to use .

If you can't jump ashore, it's possible to lasso a bollard from on deck.

Make sure one end of the line is attached to the boat!

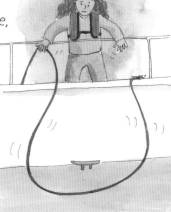

THROWING A LINE

If there is someone ashore to take your mooring line, here's how to throw it to them. Split the coil into two, one in each hand; throw the free end coil first, followed straightaway by the other one.

Oh, and don't forget to make sure your end of line is attached to the boat!

I've thrown the line, dad – now what?

COMING ALONGSIDE A GRASSY BANK

Stopping the boat along a river or canal bank is usually easy as there will be little or no current close to the bank. If there are no bollards to tie up to you'll need to use mooring stakes—make sure your mooring lines don't go across the towpath!

I'm really looking forward to this trip!

MOORING STAKES

Don't put the stake too close to the riverbank.

Angle it away from the boat for the best grip.....

GOOD IDEA

BAD IDEA

The bottom of a plastic bottle put over the stake will make it easier to see if there's a danger of people tripping over it.

ALONGSIDE A QUAY

If you're mooring to a concrete quayside, the helmsman will use the engine to stop the boat. If you're stepping ashore with mooring lines, don't try and stop it yourself - remember boats are heavy!

Wait until the boat is nearly at a stop then take a turn of the rope around a post or bollard. The friction of the post takes the strain and puts you in control.

BAD IDEA

MIND YOUR FINGERS!

GOOD IDEA

SWIGGING   No—not that sort of swigging! This is a clever way of pulling in a line that's under tension, for example when you want to pull the boat closer to the bank.

GLUG GLUG

PULL UP HERE...

MIND YOUR FINGERS!

..... THEN TAKE UP THE SLACK HERE

RAFTING UP

At busy places on rivers you may have to tie up alongside another boat. If you're the outside boat, you need to learn some boat manners.....

Coming through!

- Ask before stepping aboard (unless there's no-one there to ask!)
- Don't cross the boat with muddy or gritty shoes —take them off
- Don't peer into windows and hatches! If possible, cross over the bow rather than the cockpit
- Be good neighbours—don't play loud music late at night

HOW MOORING LINES GO.......

On a canal you need to use a bow and stern line (or for a brief stop, a centre line). On a river you'll also need spring lines to hold you against the current (you may also need these on a canal in strong winds).

BOW LINE, STERN LINE AND SPRINGS

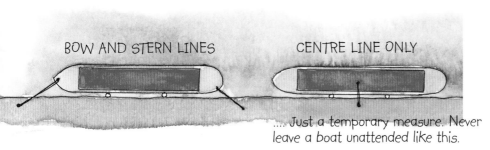

BOW AND STERN LINES

CENTRE LINE ONLY

..... Just a temporary measure. Never leave a boat unattended like this.

TYING A ROPE ONTO A CLEAT (Locking hitch)

On a motor cruiser, tie a rope onto a deck cleat like this....

1

2

3

4

Some skippers like to tie their line to a cleat with a bowline like this. Find out on the next page how to tie one.

FIGURE OF EIGHT

Use this on twin bollards like these, which are quite common in Europe. ......

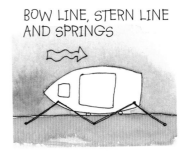

Practise rope handling techniques and knots before you need them if you want to impress your skipper!

Have you tied that bowline yet?

TEE STUD HITCH

Used for tying a mooring line to a narrowboat tee stud.

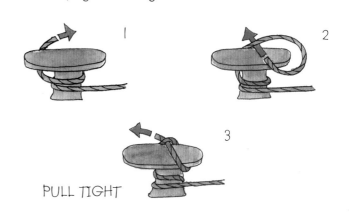

PULL TIGHT

BOWLINE

This is the knot to use when you need to make a loop in a rope. It can't be undone under load but is useful for looping a rope round a bollard.

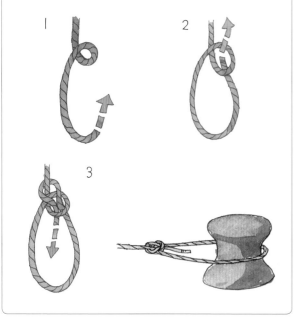

CLOVE HITCH

Here's an easy one you probably already know. This is a good one for tying a line to a mooring stake—if the stake falls into the water, the line will stay attached.

ROUND TURN AND TWO HALF HITCHES

Not just for tying on fenders, this is also useful for mooring lines as it can be released under tension.

If you can't remember how to tie it, go back to page 38.

CANALMAN'S HITCH

Useful when tying up to mooring posts or bollards.

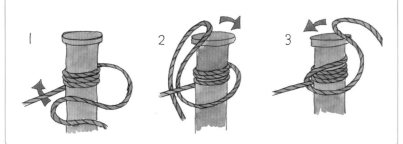

Never ever pull a rope by wrapping it round your hand or any other part of your body — you can do yourself a lot of damage!

BAD IDEA

LOCKS, BRIDGES AND TUNNELS

Chapter Five

CREW JOB LIST

Open lock gates and sluices in the right order

Handle lines in a lock without getting in a muddle

Be polite to lock keepers and other boat crews

Open and close bridges safely

Locks are like steps in a river and canal. Learning how to use a lock can sound complicated, but these are the most important things to remember...

LOCK GATES let boats in and out

A lock gate can only be opened when the water is the same level on both sides.

MORE WATER = MORE PRESSURE

SAME LEVEL = SAME PRESSURE

SLUICES (PADDLES) let water in and out

The sluices at top and bottom of the lock must never both be open at the same time!

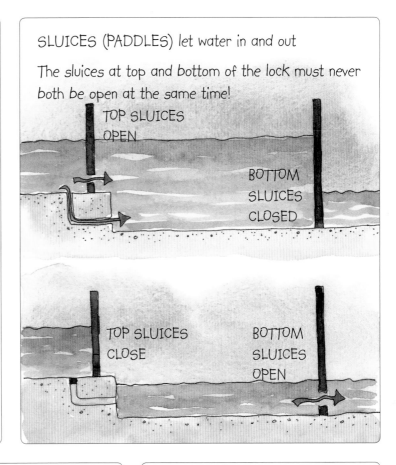

TOP SLUICES OPEN

BOTTOM SLUICES CLOSED

TOP SLUICES CLOSE

BOTTOM SLUICES OPEN

TAKE YOUR TIME

Locking takes time, so don't be impatient. You may have to wait for another boat to come through, or you may have to change the lock so that it's set in your favour.

Don't run near a lock and always wear a lifejacket. Falling into a lock is very dangerous so make sure it never ever happens to you!

BAD IDEA

DON'T WASTE WATER

Even the smallest canal lock can hold 50,000 gallons (that's nearly 200,000 litres) of water.

If a lock is set against you and there is a boat approaching from the other way, wait for them to use the lock then go in after them. Share wide locks with another boat where possible.

Some old lock gates are leaky—report any leaks or damage to waterways staff so they can be repaired.

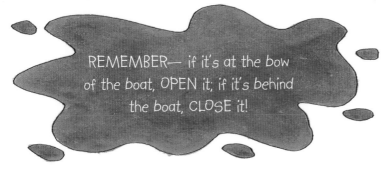

REMEMBER— if it's at the bow of the boat, OPEN it; if it's behind the boat, CLOSE it!

On the British canal system engineers tried to make locks as tiny as possible so that they didn't waste much water. That's why narrow boats are so narrow!

Narrow locks can fit a boat 6ft 10in (2.08m) wide and 70ft (21.34m) long—but only just! You'll find that your boat fits into the lock so snugly that you won't need to use mooring lines or fenders.

BALANCE BEAM

TOP GATE GROUND PADDLE

TOP (UPSTREAM) GATE

CILL

LOCK CHAMBER

BOTTOM (DOWNSTREAM) GATE

BOTTOM GATE PADDLE

BALANCE BEAM

HOW LOCK GATES OPEN

Pushing against the balance beams will gently open the gate.

Keep out of the way of balance beams when the gates are being opened!

BOTTOM GATE PADDLE

WATER WISDOM
Keep fingers and loose clothing clear of the paddle mechanism. If you've got long hair, tie it back to keep it clear!

HOW PADDLES (SLUICES) WORK

Paddles are openings inside a lock gate (or within the walls of the lock) to let the water in and out. Your boat will have a windlass like this to work the paddles.

There are several different types of paddles, and they vary from canal to canal. The best way to learn is by getting someone to show you how.

Be very careful not to leave the windlass on the paddle gear when you've finished— if the braking mechanism on the paddle failed, the handle could fly off and hurt you—or someone else. Also, you don't want to leave it behind—you'll need it for the next lock!

the lock is not already set in your favour (ready to go in), you'll be dropped off on the bank to
et it ready. Here are a few tips on how to be a good lock winder—don't forget your windlass!

GOING UPHILL—checklist

- Check that there's nobody approaching the lock from the other end.
- Make sure top gates and paddles are closed.
- Open bottom paddles gently.
- When the water has levelled, open the bottom gates.
- Once the boat is in the lock, shut bottom gates and paddles.
- Gently open top paddles, a little at first and then all the way.
- When the lock has filled, open the gates then close the paddles.
- Once the boat is out, leave the gates closed behind you unless there's a boat wanting to go in.
- The boat will pull into the bank to let you back on again.

GOING DOWNHILL—checklist

- Check that there's nobody approaching the lock from the other end.
- Make sure bottom paddles and gates are closed.
- Open the top paddles.
- When the lock has filled, close the top paddles and open the top gates for the boat to go in.
- Close the top gates.
- Open the bottom paddles, to empty the lock.
- When the water level has finished falling, open the bottom gates to let the boat out.
- While the boat is going out, close the bottom paddles. Then close the gates, unless another boat wants to come into the lock.

OPEN AND CLOSE SLUICES GENTLY

Let the water into the lock gently, or the turbulence will throw the boat around.

Open ground paddles first, then open the gate paddles once the lock is half full of water or you could flood the boat!

KEEP YOUR EYES OPEN!

Both skipper and crew need to watch out that bits of the boat, like fenders, don't get caught in the lock as the water level changes.

This locking business is really.....

Keeping the boat's bow against the lock gates should stop the stern getting caught on the cill when going downhill!

..... easy!

Bigger locks have room for more than one boat—and of course they use a lot more water, so try and share a lock with other boats where possible.

You'll need to use your mooring lines to hold the boat in place, and have the fenders ready.

A BIT TIED UP.....

Never use a knot on a lock bollard—slip the free end around it and back on board round a cleat so you can adjust it as the water level changes.

BAD IDEA

DON'T WASTE WATER!

Lock sharing means giving each other a helping hand with the gates and sluices. You'll make new friends and develop good teamwork if you do a series of locks together.

I'm not sharing a lock with those dreadful Pearsons, and that's final!

GOOD IDEA

Don't tie your lines to ladders or other fixed points on the lock walls. Think of those changing water levels! Some deep locks have vertical bars to slip your lines round so they can rise and fall with the boat.

GOOD IDEA

BAD IDEA

On rivers and bigger canals (especially the European canals), you'll find electrically operated locks. Some will open and close automatically, some will have a control panel with buttons for you to press. When there's a lock keeper, always obey his instructions!

MANNED LOCKS

If the gates are closed there will be somewhere outside the lock to moor up and wait. When the gates open the lock keeper will tell you where he wants you to go. At busy times there can be long queues at a lock, so be patient and wait for your turn. The lock keeper will try and fit as many boats in each locking as he can, arranging them by size rather than who arrived first if he needs to.

Lock keepers do more than just work the locks—they can also tell you anything you need to know about the waterways!

UNMANNED LOCKS

Bigger locks and some river locks have electric controls for the gates and sluices. Don't worry, the instructions are easy to follow!

Hmmm, this button or this one, I wonder.....?

LOCKS WITH TRAFFIC LIGHTS

If there are traffic lights at the lock gates you'll know whether you can go straight into the lock or whether you have to wait.

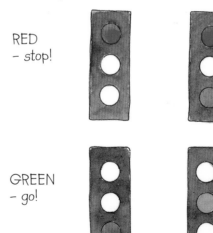

RED
- stop!

RED and GREEN
- get ready to go

GREEN
- go!

AMBER
- proceed with caution

HOLD TIGHT!

There can be a lot of turbulence in big locks, especially when they're filling.

Make sure you keep the mooring lines taut to stop the boat moving around too much, especially when the lock is full of boats.

SHIP LOCKS

On some rivers and canals, especially in Europe, there are big ship locks which will make your boat feel really small!

Traffic lights will guide you in and you may not meet the lock keeper—he'll give you instructions over a loudspeaker or VHF radio if he needs to. Some big locks are automatic and unmanned.

SHARING WITH SHIPS

Remember that working boats—cargo or passenger ships—have priority over pleasure boats (that's you). Always let commercial ships or barges go into (and out of) the lock first.

This not only gives them priority but stops little boats getting squashed by big boats!

TYING UP IN BIG LOCKS

 There may be bollards like this fixed into the lock walls for small boats to use....

...... or you may have to climb a ladder to get a mooring line ashore. Wear a lifejacket and remember that if the water level has fallen, the bottom of the ladder will be slippery!

SLIPPY BIT

BUSY LOCKS

Many big locks have floating pontoons alongside the walls for small boats to tie on to—and of course if the lock is busy you could well be tied up to another boat rather than to the lock walls—use lots of fenders and the opportunity to make new friends!

...we're going there too—we'll be able to meet up later!

FRIEND SHIP

Saucy Sue

It's not just locks that will keep you busy—canals and rivers have bridges to deal with, and some canals have tunnels too......

Wherever there are rivers and canals, there will be places where people and cars need to get cross them. You'll find more bridges on canals than on rivers, because canal builders had to build bridge every time the canal crossed a path, road or divided a farmer's land in two.

HUMPBACKED BRIDGES

Canals in the UK have lots of these traditional brick bridges, which were built as small as possible to keep costs down. Remember to keep your head down!

SWING BRIDGES

Some swing bridges are worked by hand, which may take two people. Others are powered and need a special waterways key. But don't worry, there will be clear instructions on what to do.

There may be wedges underneath at each end to stop the bridge bouncing when cars drive over. Release these before opening the bridge—and put them back again afterwards.

Remember to check for traffic and use the road barriers!

LIFTING BRIDGES

The crew's job is to prepare the bridge for the boat to pass through, but don't worry, it's not difficult! Some lifting gear will need a windlass, some will be just pulled up on a chain, but it won't feel heavy as the weight of the bridge is balanced by heavy beams.

Sit on the beam to keep the bridge open so that it doesn't fall back down and squash the boat as it goes through! Lower the bridge as gently as you can.

Remember to use the road barriers if there are any.

Bigger bridges make life easier for the crew as you don't have to open them yourselves—or if you do, it's by pushing buttons on an electric control panel. On big rivers and wide canals there will be bridges big enough for ships to get through.

SMALL BOATS AND BIG BRIDGES....

Some lifting or swing bridges are designed for big boats—these may be controlled by traffic lights, or have fixed opening times. There may be a bridgekeeper, or the opening may be automatic.

If you are small enough to pass under the bridge without it opening, you may be able to ignore the traffic lights. Be careful, though; not all bridge spans may be safe to pass through. Check your charts and check the signs on the span—in France, for example, a yellow diamond means two way traffic can pass through the span and two yellow diamonds mean one way traffic can pass through.

TUNNELS

Tunnels, like bridges, were built as small as possible to save money. If there is only room for one boat, traffic lights or instructions at the entrance will tell you if you're free to pass through. Toot your horn and put the tunnel light on before you enter.

Put some cabin lights on, and shine the tunnel light slightly upwards so that it lights up the roof of the tunnel ahead of you.

Steering in a tunnel feels very weird and it's hard to hold a steady course. Keep a point on the cabin top in line with the light at the end of the tunnel, and don't move the tiller too much. In wider tunnels, slow right down if there's a boat coming the other way.

If you're not steering, keep your arms and legs inside the boat—best of all, stay warm and dry in the cabin! And don't worry, that tunnel you're in isn't haunted—honest!

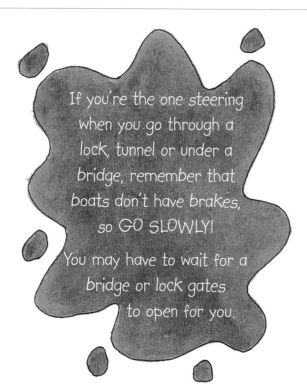

If you're the one steering when you go through a lock, tunnel or under a bridge, remember that boats don't have brakes, so GO SLOWLY!

You may have to wait for a bridge or lock gates to open for you.

What goes KCAUQ KCAUQ?

A duck flying backwards!

ARTIST ON BOARD

SHOPPING LIST

What do you do when you're off duty as crew? Don't wait for a rainy day to spend some creative time in the cabin with these arty projects.

To do all the things in this chapter, this is what you'll need:

A4 exercise book (with lined pages)
Sketch book
Thick paper or card (white or coloured)
Compasses (for the circle patterns)
Ruler, pencils, eraser
Paints (watercolour or acrylics) or crayons or felt tips
Scissors
Sticky tack or tape
Paper glue

Sir Anthony Van Duck

Whether your waterways trip lasts a day or a whole summer, it's a good idea to keep a day by day record of your journey. It will help you to remember all the places you visited.

Use a lined notebook and make a title page that looks something like this. A photo of the boat may have to wait until you're home again (unless you're cruising through towns which have a photo printing facility!)

Learn how to decorate your log book with traditional canal boat art on the next few pages.

LOG of DABCHICK

On the first page of your log book, write down all the details of your boat and her crew like this:

Boat name:

Boat length:

Type of boat:

Home mooring:

People on board:

Skipper: Crew:

Planned cruise:

Start date:
Finish date:

Inside the book, use a page (or two) for each day of your cruise. Make it as simple or as complicated as you like. Here are a few useful things to fill in each day.....

Log of "Dabchick"

Date:
From: To:
Start Time   End time:
Weather:
Distance covered:
Locks: Bridges:

Notes:

This bit can include anything you want to say about the day, including photos, drawings or postcards. Suggestions include:

- Wildlife seen today
- Jobs you've done as crew
- Different types of boat seen
- People you've met
- Unusual locks, bridges or buildings
- New boating words you've learned

THE NAME GAME

Collect boat names - try and find a name beginning with each letter of the alphabet. See who can spot the shortest (and longest) boat name. What's the funniest name you've seen today?

When British canals were at their busiest, boatmen developed a colourful way of decorating their boats and all the objects on them. Many of today's narrowboat owners like to carry on the tradition, so see how many examples of colourful canal art you can spot. Make sketches if you can, and use some of the ideas for your own projects.

If you're lucky you might see a decorative rudder like this one (especially if you go to a waterways museum). There were variations in pattern and style in different parts of the country and for different canal companies.

Canal boat decoration is not always complicated—this traditional curved design on cabin doors is still very popular.

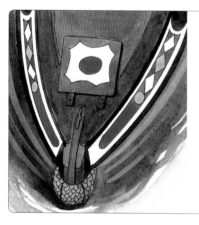

The decorative panel on a boat's bow is still very popular on canal boats. A design of circles and diamonds is the most common, often with the boat's name in the panel.

Traditional canal boat designs of roses and castles on a cabin door

Nobody knows when or why canal boat artists starting painting roses and castles, but they are still popular today.

This is called a cratch—a wooden frame supporting the canvas cover over the hold (or these days, over the cockpit). Traditionally this was painted in bright colours, or even used as advertising space by the boat company.

Families on working canal boats lived in tiny cabins, so they liked to make their few belongings as colourful as possible. Every boat had a buckby can like this for fetching water. Now they are carried just for decoration.

CHICKWEED

Look for decorative boat name panels like this one. In the days of canal trade, each company boat could be recognised by its lettering style and coloured patterns.

The next pages show you how to make some canal boat art of your own........

These simple roses have always been popular in canal boat art. They developed into a simple series of brushstrokes, which meant that artists could work quickly and save the boat owner money! Before you start on the boat, have a go in your sketchbook......

Be careful not to make a mess in the cabin—use old newspaper to protect the table.

Protect your clothes too, especially if you're using acrylic paints!

Traditionally, roses are done with enamel paints on a dark background, but you can also do them with watercolour paints on white paper, Use a soft (not bristly) paintbrush that comes to a nice point and you'll be able to do each of the petals in a single stroke......

STEP ONE
First paint a circle .....

Then use a darker colour for the petals like this.....

STEP TWO

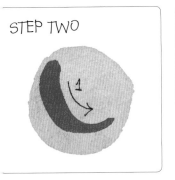

STEP THREE

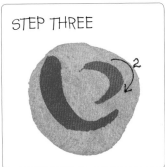

STEP FOUR

STEP FIVE

STEP SIX
Add some central strokes with a brush or pen, and suddenly your series of brushstrokes looks like a rose!

STEP SEVEN
Add a few leaf shapes like this—you should be able to do the basic shapes with two brushstrokes. Add the leaf veins with a lighter colour or felt pen.

Your finished rose should look something like this (if it doesn't, you just need more practice!)

If you have acrylic paints and dark paper or card, you can do traditional roses like this. To make the bright colours show up, paint the shape in white first. Then use a deep colour for the rose background and a lighter colour for the petals.

DAISIES are also easy to do. As they're white flowers, it's best to do them on coloured paper so that they show up. Start with a small circle of white (to make the yellow show up brighter when you add it later). Paint the first four petals (if you are using a nice soft paintbrush with a good point, you should be able to do each petal with one brushstroke). Then add two more petals in each quarter (use the numbers on a clock face as a guide). Make a garland of daisies by putting a leaf in between each one.

Using the basic four pointed daisy as a starting point, you can make all sorts of patterns. Copy these or design your own. It's a good idea to draw some guidelines in pencil to help you keep the designs nice and even. Don't forget to rub the guidelines out afterwards.

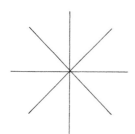

If you're not keen on flowers, here's another design based on a circle that was often found on barge rudders. You'll need a pair of compasses to do this one—make sure you don't squeeze them while you're making the pattern!

1
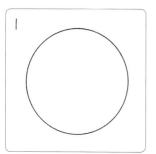

2
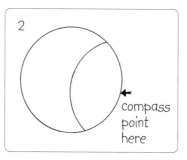
compass point here

3
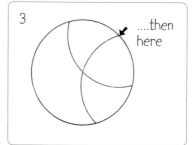
....then here

4
.... then here, and so on
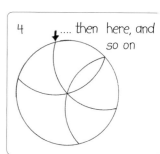

5
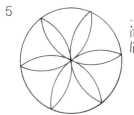
.... until it looks like this

6
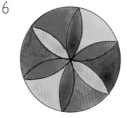

When colouring or painting the design, use bright colours and put the colours opposite each other like this...

Always put compasses and scissors away carefully when you've finished and don't leave them lying around—especially on a moving boat!

This is a traditional canal boat alphabet. Use this for your name panel by tracing or copying the letters you need.

Use the letters with or without the shadow bit—but if you draw the shadow, make sure you make it a darker colour than the rest.

Canal art is traditionally used to decorate boats and all the objects on them, but there's no reason why you can't use paper and paint too. Here's how to make a name panel for your cabin door.....

STEP ONE
Sketch out your design on scrap paper or in your sketch book first.

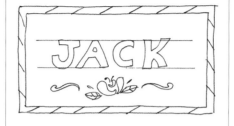

STEP TWO
Do the lettering first, in the middle of a page, between two ruled lines. Then put a centre line down the page lightly in pencil—this will help you keep your design balanced.

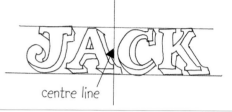

centre line

STEP THREE
Use a ruler to draw the border. Make sure your centre line is still the middle point and leave enough space around the lettering for any designs you want to paint.

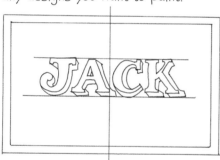

BORDERS
If you want to use a striped or diamond border, you'll need to make equal measurements so that the shapes are all even, like this.....

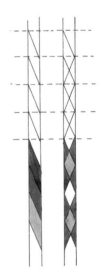

.... or use your paintbrush to do a string of simple loops and garlands like this......

Add some roses, daisies or other designs if you want to, rub out the pencil marks, cut out the finished panel and stick it on your cabin door (use sticky tack or similar—don't use anything that will leave a mark on the door!)

What do you call four ducks in a box?

A box of quackers!

WATERWAYS LIFE

WATCH OUT!

If you're not steering the boat or busy in the cabin, there's nothing to do, right? Wrong! Use your eyes, know what to look for and there's plenty to discover, from rare animals like otters to clues about the waterway's busy cargo carrying past.

But first, a few words on how to look after the waterways and help to keep them special......

Ah yes, humans – they migrate here in large numbers at this time of year.....

veryone who enjoys the waterways can play a
art in making them a great place to be, not
st for people but for everything that lives
here. Here are some things you can do to help.

OUT OF SIGHT, OUT OF MIND?

Never, ever throw rubbish into the water. No, not even if
it's biodegradable, like food scraps.

Be especially careful not to let plastic bags blow over the
side—it's not only really bad for wildlife but can also get
jammed in a boat's propeller. More than a million birds
and animals die every year from accidentally eating or
getting tangled up in plastic waste.

GET DOWN AND DIRTY.....

If you want to get involved in clearing and restoring
canals, there is still plenty of work to be done. If you are
18 or over, join a canal camp organised by the Waterway
Recovery Group (www.wrg.org.uk). You don't have to have
a special skill as training will be given; just be prepared
to work hard and you'll have fun too. Canal camps can
also count towards your Duke of Edinburgh award.

KEEP IT CLEAN!

Cruisers and canal boats have holding tanks
for toilets which can be safely pumped out,
but waste water from sinks and showers
goes straight into the water. Try not to use
too much soap or shampoo and choose
environmentally friendly cleaning products
wherever you can. Avoid bleach, chlorine and
phosphates in particular.

Don't let oil or engine fuel leak into the
water—be a good crew and learn how to
check the drip tray under the engine and
gearbox.

TURN IT DOWN!

Noise can be damaging to wildlife, as well as
annoying for other river users. If you want to
listen to music, keep the volume down or use
earphones.

The waterways are home for all sorts of small animals and birds. Many are very shy and you'll need to be still and quiet to spot them. Binoculars are useful as most wild creatures won't let you get too close.

Respect all wildlife and its habitat. Birds and animals have their home on the waterways—you are just a visitor!

CHOOSING BINOCULARS

Binoculars have numbers marked on them—8x30 means that the binoculars magnify eight times and the widest lenses are 30mm across. Big lenses let more light in, but you don't want to carry binoculars which are too heavy. A lightweight pair of 8x30 which fit in your pocket would be good for wildlife watching.

That's just a common duck!

Keep the safety strap on so they don't fall in the water!

Who are you calling common?

WILDLIFE WATCHER'S CODE

• Don't cause distress to wild creatures. Watch quietly from a distance, and be especially careful around nesting birds at the water's edge.

• If you want to catch small creatures like insects to study them, be careful not to damage them. Carefully let them go again when you've finished looking at them.

• Try not to disturb hedges, river banks and grass more than you can help. If you turn over a stone to look at the creatures underneath, always turn it back again.

• Don't wander onto private land without asking permission.

• Leave everywhere as you found it. Don't drop litter!

Use a notebook or your logbook to write notes about what you see, and if possible do a sketch as well.

The next few pages show you a few of the wild creatures who make their home along canals and rivers. See how many you can spot during your cruise......

veryone knows what a duck looks like—but take a
loser look and you'll see many different sorts of wild
ucks and other waterfowl.....

Don't feed wild ducks with
human food, however much
they beg you to! It's like
junk food—low in nutrients
it fills them up but makes
them too ill to survive
properly in the wild.

MALLARD
The most common and well loved ducks of all,
domesticated ducks are descended from wild mallards
like this. The male is the one with the bright colours,
and the female is a dull brown.

Mallards are very
friendly, but don't
be tempted to
feed them bread
scraps; it's not
good for them!

GREY HERON
Usually seen
standing quite
still at the
water's edge
waiting patiently
to dive for a fish.

Herons are big
birds and their
nests can be
up to a metre
across!

SWAN
Another familiar sight, the
mute swan is quite tame and
may tap on your boat's hull at
meal times hoping for a snack!

Be firm, don't feed them and
keep your fingers well clear of
their beaks!

MOORHEN
Looks very similar to a coot, but with a
bright red and yellow bill and a white stripe
down the side of the body.

Moorhens are very defensive of their
territory and will
make a noisy fuss
if any other creature
tries to get near.

COOT
Coots are easy to spot because of their white bill and
black feathers, and although usually in groups, they're very
noisy and quarrelsome!

They are not graceful birds—watch them take off by
running noisily along the
surface of the water or
bobbing back to the
surface after catching a fish!

Most wild birds are very shy, and remember that they often make their nests on the river or canal bank. Be careful where you tread as nests are not easy to see. Don't get too close to birds on a nest and be as quiet as you can.

Stay away from our nests or you'll frighten our babies.

PRIVATE

GREBE
Another small bird, with distinctive golden tufts on its head. In the winter its coat turns to light grey.

DABCHICK
This one is really tiny— duck shaped but with almost no tail, and feathers turn to light colours in the winter.

PINTAIL
The male and female have very different colours but both have long pointed tail feathers, especially the male.

KINGFISHER

This small but colourful bird is exciting to see—and you often only get a flash of colour as it dives for a fish. Very sensitive to water pollution, the presence of Kingfishers is a good sign as it means clean water. Avoid getting too close to a Kingfisher nest as this can make them abandon their babies!

There is a legend about Kingfishers which explains their Greek name HALCYON. The Greek goddess Alcyone, daughter of the wind, was so grief stricken when her husband drowned in a shipwreck that she threw herself into the sea. Both she and her husband were then magically turned into Kingfishers so they could roam the sea together. Alcyone's father, Aeolus the god of wind, made sure the weather was always calm and gentle when they made their nest, so the saying 'Halcyon Days' has come to mean calm or peaceful times.

BLACK HEADED GULL
Gulls are usually found on the coast, but quite a few, like this black headed gull, are seen on lakes and rivers too.

Gulls will eat anything —fish, worms, insects, rubbish, or your lunch, so don't leave your food out on deck!

nimals will be harder to spot as they are all very shy and you may only see the flick of a tale as hey run away or dive underwater. Here are a few of the most likely riverbank creatures, if you're cky enough to see some, and a few of our favourite insects......

WATER SHREW

A very small animal that likes to eat quite big things including insects, fish and even frogs. It uses poisonous saliva to kill its prey.

WATER VOLE

Bigger than the shrew at 16-19cm, water voles are quite rare because of loss of habitat and the increase of mink, who find voles a tasty snack. Voles live in burrows in the river or canal bank. They don't have webbed feet but swim in a slow doggy-paddle style. They eat grasses, nuts and roots and sometimes leave piles of neatly chopped grass at the entrance to their burrows.

'Ratty' in the famous story Wind in the Willows was a water vole!

MINK

Not a native in Europe, the American mink was bred in farms for its fur and has since become established in the wild. It's a bold hunter and good swimmer, likes to eat fish and small animals - especially voles!

OTTER

One of the best loved river creatures but quite rare because of habitat destruction and water pollution. Otters eat fish as well as small animals like voles. Very timid and hard to spot.

DRAGONFLY AND DAMSELFLY

It's hard to tell the dragonfly and damselfly apart, but damselflies are smaller and daintier. They can fly at up to 30mph and create a flash of colour on water as they hunt other small creatures. They are not shy and if you're careful and gentle you may get one to sit on your finger!

EMPEROR
DRAGONFLY

RED DAMSELFLY

BLUE
DAMSELFLY

BAT

Bats like to fly around at dusk and catch insects, using a clever form of radar to fly without bumping into everything. They live in quiet dark places like empty buildings and under canal bridges.

The tiny pipistrelle bat is 3-5cm long with about 20cm wingspan.

There are plenty of clues on rivers and canals that tell the story of their horse drawn and cargo carrying days. Give yourself ten points for each one you discover, and if you have other members o your crew watching too, whoever spots it first gets the points!

TOWROPE TRAIL

Look carefully at old stone bridges and you might see deep grooves worn by all the towropes of horse drawn boats. Sometimes the canal company put a metal post on the corners to protect the brickwork.

Old wooden bollards have grooves cut by mooring lines, especially near locks where engineless boats used ropes to pull them in and out of the lock. If you're using one of these bollards, make sure your ropes don't get caught in the grooves!

Blind bends can be a problem for narrowboats today —but they wouldn't have been a problem for a horse drawn barge because the horseman would be far enough ahead to see what was coming. O sharp bends a wooden roller like this would guide the towline round

CLEVER BRIDGES

Can you work out why a bridge might have a gap in the middle like this? If the towpath changed from one side of the canal to the other, the horse could go over the bridge and down to the other side while the tow rope was dropped through the gap in the bridge. This saved time because it meant that the towline didn't have to be untied as the horse changed sides.

SPLIT BRIDGE

TURNOVER BRIDGE

Here's another clever design to stop the towline being unhitched when the horse crosses over from one side of the canal to the other. Follow the path over the bridge and work out how the horse was able to change sides without getting the towrope in a tangle.

LOCK KEEPER'S COTTAGE

Although most small locks are now unmanned, you'll usually find a cottage nearby where the lock keeper and his family lived in the busy days of commercial trade. Coal for his fire would come from passing boats, probably in exchange for vegetables grown in his garden. The job of keeper would be passed down from father to son.

MILESTONES

Canal companies used to charge a toll for using the waterways, so milestones were important for working out how much to charge. They were made of stone or metal, so many are still around today.

WHARF CRANE

These were once found wherever boats loaded and unloaded their cargo. There are still the remains of a few left on the canal banks.

PUBS AND STABLES

Pubs have always been important to waterways — a place for boatmen to meet their friends, exchange news and find out about available jobs and cargo. If you stop at a waterways pub (they are often conveniently close to locks), see if it still has buildings which used to be stables for the horses that pulled the boats.

BOLLARDS AND RINGS

See how many different types of mooring bollards and rings you can find on quaysides old and new........

WAREHOUSES

If you're cruising through towns and cities, keep an eye open for waterside buildings that used to be warehouses, mills or factories.

They're likely to be apartments, offices or shops now, but many of them will have clues to their history—look for loading bays and remains of cranes above the water.

Test your knowledge of waterways words by ticking the correct choice of answer — then try them out on your family. Check your answers in the Water Words section at the end of the book.

What is a GONGOOZLER?

A) A rare species of duck

B) Someone who watches the boats go by (usually at locks)

C) A pole used for pushing boats off the mud

GONGOOZLER?

goozle! goozle!

What would you put in a WINDING HOLE?

A) Your windlass

B) Your rubbish

C) Your boat (when you want to turn and go in the other direction)

WINDING HOLE?

Where would you use a CRATCH for?

A) Holding up the cockpit cover

B) Holding up the helmsman's trousers

C) Scratching an itch you can't reach

What is a BUTTY?

A) Something you eat

B) A good mate

C) An engineless barge towed astern

BUTTY?

mmmm!

BALANCE BEAM?

What is a BALANCE BEAM for?

A) Opening lock gates

B) Improving your balance

C) Checking how much you've got in the bank

What would you put in a HOLDING TANK?

A) Drinking water

B) Bath water

C) Poo!

What is a RUBBING STRAKE for?

A) Cleaning the boat

B) Protecting the boat's hull from damage

C) Scratching an itch you can't reach

What is meant by a boat's DRAUGHT?

A) The depth of the hull below the waterline

B) The fresh air flowing through the cabin

C) How wide she is

aaah!

CRATCH OR RUBBING STRAKE?

EXTREME ENGINEERING

This chapter is about some of the biggest, most impressive and cleverest waterway engineering in the world - just in case there's anyone left in your family who thinks waterways are a bit tame! You'll also find out about a canal that put pirates out of business and how a naked Greek scientist paved the way for the invention of boat lifts......

Prepare to have your mind stre......tched!

Locks work well but they're slow and use a lot of water. As canals got busier, engineers found cleverer ways to move boats between levels. BOAT LIFTS raise and lower boats using two counterbalanced tanks (called CAISSONS), so the weight of the tank going down causes the other tank to rise, like a seesaw. Here are some famous boat lifts, new and old....

THE FALKIRK WHEEL

Completed in 2002, the Falkirk Wheel links the Forth & Clyde canal with the Union Canal in Scotland. It raises and lowers boats 24 metres using two tanks which are at each end of a large wheel. One tank goes up as the other comes down, and the wheel is so well balanced that it takes very little energy to turn. Very impressive and well worth a visit!

This boat goes up.....

..... while this boat goes down

THE ANDERTON BOAT LIFT in Cheshire was built in 1875 to raise boats from the River Weaver to the Trent and Mersey Canal. In 2002 it was restored, converted from steam to electric power, and is now in full working order again.

In 1882 engine failure caused one of the tanks (with a boat in!) to fall 50'(over 15metres). No lasting damage was done but it must have given the boatmen a shock!

A recently built boat lift is the STREPY-THIEU LIFT on the Canal du Centre in Belgium. At a height of over 73 metres, it is the tallest boat lift in Europe.

One for the scientists....... Which is heavier, a tank of water with a boat in or a tank of water without a boat in?

Answer on the next page

Another kind of boat lift is called an INCLINED PLANE. The boat goes into a watertight tank, the gates are shut behind it and the tank is pulled up a slope to the next level. Like boat lifts, inclined planes used two tanks to balance each other, which meant they only needed a small steam engine to move them. Modern day inclined planes use electricity, of course.

FOXTON INCLINE in Leicestershire carried the boat tanks sideways from one level to another. Opened in 1900, it meant that a boat could change level in about 12 minutes instead of queueing for the flight of 10 Foxton locks. It worked well for about 10 years then the railways made canal cargo uneconomic so it was abandoned.

Foxton locks are still worth a visit, and restoration plans mean that one day the Foxton incline may be fully working again!

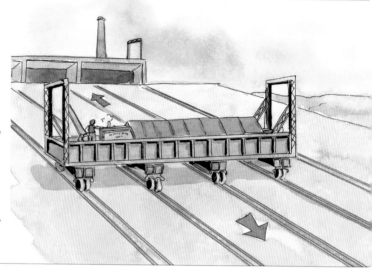

RONQUIERES INCLINED PLANE on the Brussels-Charleroi canal in Belgium is massive! It lifts boats through 68 metres in huge tanks 91 metres long and 12 metres wide that can carry several boats. The tanks are winched up and down by 8 cables, and the journey between the two levels takes 45 minutes.

The lift uses wedge shaped caissons to keep the water level steady up and down the slope.

The simplest form of incline can sometimes be seen alongside a lock—a set of rollers to pull dinghies and canoes up.

Faster, faster!

ANSWER TO THE QUESTION ON THE PREVIOUS PAGE.....

Archimedes was an ancient Greek brain box who discovered lots of amazing things about maths and science. Playing in his bath one day he realised that the amount of water displaced by an object (like a boat) was equal to the weight of the object (boat).... Which means the heavier the boat, the more water has to move out of the way to make room for it.

So, thanks to Archimedes, canal engineers centuries later knew that a tank with a boat in would weigh the same as a tank without a boat. This meant that two tanks in a lift could balance each other perfectly, with or without a boat in!

The story goes that Archimedes was so excited by this discovery that he jumped out of the bath and ran down the street shouting Eureka! (which is Greek for "I have found it!") The trouble was, he completely forgot to get dressed.......

Canals don't just join up rivers, they can connect oceans too. Travelling by canals may seem slow, but canals that make a short cut for sea going ships can cut weeks off a long voyage. Let's start with the most famous one of all.......

THE PANAMA CANAL

connects the Atlantic and Pacific oceans. Look at a globe or atlas and you'll see how much of a short cut it is for ships travelling between the two oceans. Before the canal was built, a ship had to risk the most dangerous sea passage of all—stormy Cape Horn, at the bottom of South America. Canal building started in 1880 but it was such a difficult job that it wasn't finished until 1914!

The canal is now busier than ever with boats from the biggest cargo ships (called Panamax, the biggest size to fit in a lock) to small yachts.

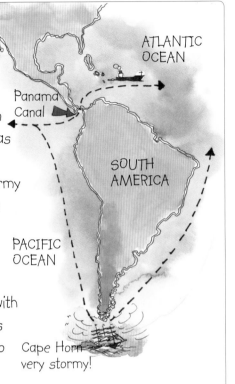

ATLANTIC OCEAN

Panama Canal

SOUTH AMERICA

PACIFIC OCEAN

Cape Horn very stormy!

The lock gates at Panama's Gatun locks are made of steel, 2 metres thick and 20 metres high! You'd need a very big balance beam to open that by hand.......

THE SUEZ CANAL

THE SUEZ CANAL links the Mediterranean and Red Sea, which means that boats don't have to go all the way round Africa, another long and stormy passage. Ancient Egyptians were the first to dig a canal at Suez, but the modern day canal is busier than ever with boats of all sizes.

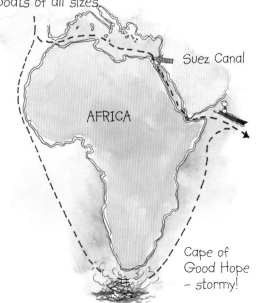

Suez Canal

AFRICA

Cape of Good Hope - stormy!

THE CALEDONIAN CANAL

THE CALEDONIAN CANAL cuts 100 km across Scotland from east to west. It's really a series of small canals which join up four lochs (lakes), including the famous Loch Ness. The lochs are part of the Great Glen, a crack in the earth's crust. Thomas Telford built the canal, but it was never very busy with big ships as it was too shallow in places.

By the time it had been made deeper, the railways had been built and taken the canal's cargo trade. But the canal is popular again today with pleasure boats enjoying the spectacular scenery.

You don't believe all that Loch Ness monster nonsense do you, Mavis?

Europe has a big network of canals; if you look at the map on the inside back cover you'll see that waterways link up most European countries. If you had plenty of time and the right boat you could begin your journey in France and finish in Romania! Here are a few interesting tales about one of the most popular canals, which is also the oldest working canal in Europe.......

THE CANAL DU MIDI in France forms part of the 'Canal des Deux Mers' which means 'canal of the two seas', a useful short cut between the bay of Biscay and the Mediterranean. In early days this saved time, money and lives — not only was the Bay of Biscay famous for storms and pirates, but the Spanish who controlled the Straits of Gibraltar levied heavy taxes on boats coming into the Mediterranean.

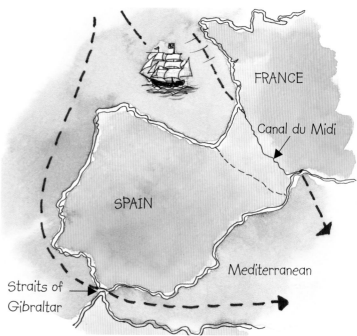

Business has been really bad since they built the canal....

The canal opened in 1681, after 12 years digging. Today it is busier than ever, with leisure boaters enjoying the beautiful tree lined banks and sea going yachts taking the short cut to and from the Mediterranean.

The 160m long MALPAS TUNNEL on the Canal du Midi was one of the earliest canal tunnels ever built. In the 17th century no-one had ever tried to take a canal through a hill, but canal engineer Riquet decided to try and cut through the crumbling rock. Riquet's bosses ordered him to stop and shut down the site as they thought it was too dangerous, but Riquet gathered his workers and carried on quickly in secret. Luckily he finished the tunnel and proved it could be done— and it's still in use today.

Summers are very hot in the south of France, so trees were planted along the canal to provide shade and stop too much water evaporating! It also made life more pleasant for the boatmen and their horses along the towpath.

How to make the most of inland waters

Don't rush—especially at locks. Think before you act.

Keep a good lookout when the boat's moving—especially if you're steering!

Be water wise—wear a lifejacket and move around the boat carefully.

Keep arms and legs inboard, especially at locks, tunnels and when coming alongside.

Look after the waterways—don't throw litter in or around the water, ever.

Research the area you're cruising and find interesting places to visit along the way.

Keep a log book

Practise knot tying

The section on 'Learn the Language' in Chapter One will help you get to know what most things are called on a boat. Here's a useful guide to all sorts of new words you might come across on your cruise.....

Aqueduct	Bridge carrying a canal over a river or road
Balance beam	Wooden bar that you push against to open lock gates
Bilges	Underneath the floor of the boat
Bollard	Post on the quayside for tying your mooring lines to
Bow	Front of the boat
Buckby can	Traditional water carrying can used on canal boats
Bulkhead	Dividing wall between cabins
Buoy	Floating marker – either for navigation or for tying a boat to
Butty	An engineless cargo boat towed behind or alongside a canal boat (or something tasty between two slices of bread.....)
Cabin sole	Floor of the cabin
Cleat	Metal fitting on the deck to tie mooring lines to
Coach roof	Roof of the cabin
Cratch	Traditionally a frame to support a canvas cover over the cargo; these days it supports an awning over the cockpit or foredeck
Cut	Traditional word for canal
Draught	Depth of boat below the waterline
Fairlead	Metal fitting on the gunwale to help a rope lead smoothly from boat to shore
Fender	squidgy plastic cushion to protect the boat's sides against a quay (often made of rope on a narrowboat's bow and stern)
Galley	Boaty word for kitchen
Gongoozler	Onlookers who watch the boats, especially at locks
Gunwale	Edge of the hull
Holding Tank	Where the contents of the toilet go. (sometimes the term is also used for the water tank – don't get the two mixed up!)
Hull	Main shell of the boat – the bit that floats!
Knot	Not just something you tie in a rope, the speed of a boat is measured in knots (nautical miles per hour) on most rivers and on tidal waters
Legger	Man who had the job of lying on his back and walking an unpowered boat through a tunnel
Lock	Way of getting boats through changes of level in a canal

BUCKBY CAN

CLEAT

FAIRLEAD

MOORING STAKE

Mooring stake	Bigger than a tent peg – used for tying mooring lines onto a grassy bank
Narrowboat	Long and narrow boat designed for the narrow canals of the British waterways
Navigation	Another word for canal or navigable river
Paddle	(also sluice) Small door in a lock gate or at the side of a lock to let water through
Port	Left hand side (usually used on rivers or tidal waters)
Pound	Stretch of water between two locks
Pulpit	Safety rail on the bow of a cruiser
Rubbing strake	Protective band around the hull of a boat like a car bumper
Rudder	Connected to the tiller, determines the direction of the boat
Side pond	Reservoirs at the side of a lock, particularly on a flight of locks, to help conserve water
Sluice	(see paddle)
Staircase lock	Series of locks where the top gate of one lock is the bottom gate of another
Starboard	Right hand side (usually used on rivers or tidal waters)
Stern	Back of the boat
Stern button	Fender at the stern of a narrowboat (protects the rudder)
Stern dolly	Mooring post or tee stud at the stern of a narrowboat
Swigging	Pulling on a rope by leaning your weight on it then taking up the slack
Tee stud	Post on a narrowboat for tying mooring lines to
Tiller	Attached to the rudder – used to steer the boat
Towpath	Runs alongside a canal or river – used originally for the horses that pulled the boats
Turnover bridge	Also called a snake bridge – changes the towpath from one side to another without the towrope having to be unhitched from the horse.
Weir	Controls the flow of water on a river – there will be a lock close by for boats to get past
Well Deck	Front cockpit of a narrowboat
Winding Hole	Turning space on a canal
Windlass	Metal lever for opening and closing sluices (paddles)

PULPIT

TEE STUD

WINDLASS

Signs which give you information..........

Water	Refuse disposal	Mooring (may have time limit)	Winding point	Tunnel	Turning place

Lifting bridge	Elsan point	Toilets	Toilet pump out

A red circle with a red line tells you what you can't do.....

No entry	No overtaking	No anchoring	No mooring	No pump out

No refuse disposal	No turning	Do not create wash	No fishing	No motor boats

Warning signs, and signs which tell you what you must do......

Beware	Sound horn	Speed limit	One way	Cross over channel

Keep to the left side of channel	Keep to right side of channel	Limited headroom	Limited depth	Limited width

Ferry	Weir	Overhead Cable		Move over or turn in this direction

Sound signals

One short blast	I am turning to the right (starboard)	Two short blasts	I am turning to the left (port)
Three short blasts	My engines are going astern	One long blast	Warning at tunnels, blind bends, junctions

Five or more short blasts   Your intentions are unclear/you are not getting out of my way fast enough!

Four short blasts, pause, one short blast   I am turning 180 degrees to the right (starboard)

Four short blasts, pause, two short blasts   I am turning 180 degrees to the left (port)

Royal Yachting Association www.rya.org.uk	RYA House, Ensign Way, Hamble, Southampton, Hants SO31 4YA
British Marine Federation www.britishmarine.co.uk	Trade association for the marine industry, includes career advice and Schools Marine Challenge
The Green Blue www.thegreenblue.org.uk	Find out how to make your boating more environmentally friendly
Inland Waterways Association www.waterways.org.uk	Association to promote the use, maintenance and restoration of Britain's inland waterways. PO Box 114, Rickmansworth, WD3 1ZY
Environment Agency www.environment-agency.gov.uk	Governing body for protecting the environment. Comprehensive website with useful information and guides for waterway users.
www.waterscape.com	British Waterways' leisure website—a comprehensive guide to rivers, lakes and canals in the UK. Includes interactive games and the opportunity to register rare wildlife you've spotted.
www.thewaterwaystrust.org.uk	The Waterways Trust website
www.wow4water.net	Wild Over Waterways website, specially for children. Interactive games and activities
www.wrg.org.uk	Waterways Recovery Group — co-ordinates volunteers to restore Britain's derelict waterways
www.canaljunction.com	Cruising guide to British Inland Waterways
www.mike-stevens.co.uk	Campaigning to preserve British waterways
Association of Pleasure Craft www.apco.org.uk	Directory of all sorts of hire boat companies for days out and holidays, also Operators. Includes games to play
www.barges.org	The Barge Association (formerly Dutch Barge Association), for European waterways cruisers and barge enthusiasts
www.riverthames.co.uk	Comprehensive guide to the River Thames and connected waterways
www.environment-agency.gov.uk/regions/thames	Find out more about the Thames Flood Barrier
www.canalcargo.co.uk	Canal Cargo Internet Bookshop, Stockists of inland waterways publications
www.tradline.co.uk	Tradline Ropes & Fenders. Mail order and Internet supplier of fenders, rope and lots more

Waterways Museums and Attractions

River and Rowing Museum, Henley on Thames www.rrm.co.uk	The Anderton Boat Lift www.andertonboatlift.co.uk
Canal du Midi www.canal-du-midi.org	The Falkirk Wheel www.thefalkirkwheel.co.uk
National Waterways Museum has three locations: www.nwm.org.uk and www.boatmuseum.org.uk	Gloucester Docks, Ellesmere Port and Stoke Bruerne

Index

83